CORNERSTONES
for
Writing

Pupil's Book
Year 4

**Alison Green, Jill Hurlstone
and Jane Woods**

Series Editor
Jean Glasberg

CAMBRIDGE
UNIVERSITY PRESS

Five steps to GOOD WRITING

1 **Modelling:** use a model text to help you learn how to write your own text

Use the activities in this book

2 **Plan your own text**

Use the planning frames or the activities in this book

3 **Draft your text**

Work on your own text

4 **Revise and edit your text**

Work on your own text

5 **Publish your text**

Work on your own text

 When you see this symbol, do this activity with a partner or in a group.

CONTENTS

1 How to write

a historical story

1 Looking at the story structure

1 The story of *A Camp to Hide King Alfred* has got mixed up. In your book, write out these sentences in the right order.

Then draw boxes round the beginning, middle and end sections.

During a feast, a man arrived with torn clothes. He said that the Vikings had attacked the King.

The King came out of hiding.

Wulfric had a hideaway in the marshes. He wanted to be a soldier in King Alfred's army.

Wulfric became a sea soldier.

Wulfric hid on a cart and went to fight with the King.

There was a battle. The Saxons beat the Vikings.

Wulfric took the King to his hiding place.

King Alfred made peace with the Vikings.

The Vikings looked for the King.

Now tell the story to your partner.

2 Read this story with your partner. Use **copymaster 1** to write down the main events. Mark the **problem**, **climax** and **resolution**. This will give you a story plan for *The Saga of Leif Erikson*.

The Saga of Leif Erikson

Beginning

On a frosty February night, in a wooden hut just above a Norwegian fjord*, a woman known as Gudrid gave birth to a son.

There was no rejoicing. The baby was a puny-looking thing and as pale as a trussed-up chicken waiting for the spit.

The father, known as Erik the Red, turned his head away in disappointment and disgust.

*a long, narrow arm of sea between high cliffs

Middle

"You know what you must do," he muttered to his wife's slave-woman. The family's dog whined in the corner.

Straight away, the slave-woman grabbed the baby from its sobbing mother and stepped out of the hut. Only then did she wrap the baby in her cloak. She walked towards the mountainside. The dog went with her.

Then the slave-woman placed the baby by a ragged gorse bush on the wildest part of the mountain. She left it there for the wolves, as is the Viking custom.

She called the dog to follow her back to their mistress's hut. The dog growled and lay down with its paws outstretched. It would not follow her. "The Lord keep you," she whispered, for, unlike her Viking mistress, she was a Christian.

End

Next morning, old Olaf, the blind bone-carver, heard the sound of crying coming from a gorse bush.

He found the baby, hungry but warm enough, snuggled like a young pup under the belly of the dog. Neither dog nor baby had been troubled by wolves.

Gudrid wept when the old man brought in the baby.
"It is the will of the gods that the child shall live," declared Erik. "Let him be known by the name Leif."

From *The Saga of Leif Erikson* by Roy Apps

3 Look at this plan for the beginning and end of a story.
Plan the middle section, including a climax.

Beginning
Saxon girls Drifa and her sister Mary are weaving
cloth at their home in Chippenham.

Problem:
The Vikings attack, their house is burned and they
can't find the rest of their family.

Middle

Conflict/Climax:

End
The house is rebuilt.

Resolution:
Drifa and Mary find their family.

Now take it in turns to tell the story to your partner.

2 Showing the passing of time in a story

1 Read these time phrases. Use **copymaster 2** and write each phrase in the correct box.

> For a few minutes…
> After three days of wild wind…
> Darkness had fallen…
> A month later…
> As the days went by…
> Summer changed to autumn…
> The years slipped by…
> Two hours later…
> The sun rose in the sky…
> May became June…

Try to find some more in your reading book, or make up some of your own.

2 Here are some time phrases from real stories. Use **copymaster 2** and write each phrase in the correct box.

> The first chill light of dawn…
> Within one minute…
> The sun had completed its journey across the sky…
> As the first flowers were beginning to bloom…
> In the seventh week after Easter…
> One full moon later…
> As the damp greyness of winter gave way to spring…
> On a frosty February night…
> They walked into the gathering dark…
> He had changed from a boy to a man…

Now use the copymaster to make up some more time phrases of your own.

1 Look at this picture of the
Saxon hall in the story. Write down
the different objects you can see.
Then write what the people are doing.

Think of the smells and sounds in the hall.
Write these down as well.

2 Look at the pictures. Write a description of *either* the village *or* the hall on page 8. Include details about the objects you can see and the different smells and sounds.

3 Look at the pictures. Choose *either* the hall on page 8 *or* the village. Imagine that you are a Saxon 'tour-guide' showing people around. They want to know what everything is and what it is like to live here. Write down what you will tell them.

Choose one of these characters. This is going to be the main character for your story.

- Think of a name for your character.
- What does your character look like?
- What is he or she wearing?
- What kind of person do you think your character is?

1 Use **copymaster 3** to write a character profile.

2 Write a character profile for your character. Set it out like this in your book:

(Draw a picture of your character here.)

Name _____

Age _____

Address _____

_____

Family _____

_____

Appearance

_____

_____

_____

Interests/hobbies

_____

_____

_____

_____

Personality

_____

_____

_____

_____

_____

ADDITIONAL SESSIONS

Writing a diary entry for a historical character

1 Choose the word which you think best describes Wulfric's feelings.

Copy out and complete the sentences in your book.

1 At the feast Wulfric felt ⟨ sad cheerful upset ⟩ because _____.

2 When he took the King to his hideout, Wulfric felt ⟨ worried happy cross ⟩ because _____.

3 When Wulfric's father said that he couldn't be in the army, Wulfric felt ⟨ glad angry cheated ⟩ because _____.

4 When he fought the Vikings, Wulfric felt ⟨ proud tired scared ⟩ because _____.

5 When he became a sea soldier, Wulfric was ⟨ excited nervous sad ⟩ because _____.

2 Decide whether you are going to be Eadgifu or Wulfric. Copy one of the charts below into your book and fill it in, describing your character's feelings.

Use the words at the bottom to help you. Look them up in a thesaurus and find some more interesting words.

Wulfric

Events	Feelings
In the den	
Hides the King	
Stopped from being a soldier	
Fights in battle	
Becomes a sea soldier	

Eadgifu

Events	Feelings
At the feast	
Wulfric hides the King	
Wulfric is stopped from going to battle. Eadgifu helps him.	
Wulfric fights in the battle	
Wulfric becomes a sea soldier	

Useful words

happy	upset	sad	scared	angry	excited	worried

Writing a playscript from the story

1 Work with a partner. Copy this framework into your book. Use it to write the first two scenes of *A Camp to Hide King Alfred*.

Scene 1: An island in the Somerset marshes

(*It is sunset. Wulfric is alone in his hideaway among the reeds and rushes.*)

Wulfric: _____
_____
_____

Scene 2: The hall in the village

(_____)

Aelfwin: _____
Wulfric: _____
Eadgifu: _____
Wulfric: _____
Wynflaed: _____
Everyone: _____

2 Read this section of *A Camp to Hide King Alfred*.
Turn it into a playscript. Use **copymaster 5** to make a plan.
Then write the playscript and perform it with your friends.

Wulfric's father Aelfwin was master of the hall. He took the youth, Wynflaed, to the bower to speak with him alone, but Wulfric followed them.

"The King is in great danger, we must find him a place to hide," Wynflaed whispered urgently.

"I know the very place," said Wulfric as he strode into the bower. They all agreed that Wulfric should show Wynflaed's riding companion, Hereberht, where the place was so that he could decide if it was fit for a king.

It was cold, dark and foggy as Wulfric and Hereberht rowed across the water to Wulfric's camp. When they arrived, Hereberht took off his glove and showed Wulfric his ring; it said *Alfred Rex*. He was the King!

When Wulfric arrived home, the first chill light of dawn had already broken through the sky. Wynflaed gave the boy the job of taking food to the King.

Later that morning on the edge of the marsh, he was stopped by Vikings on horseback. "Where y'going boy?" they demanded.

"To my castle," replied Wulfric, and the Vikings guffawed with laughter and rode away.

3 Re-read your story with a historical setting. Turn it into a playscript.

Use **copymaster 5** to plan it.

Think carefully about these questions:

- How many scenes will you need?

- Who are the characters?

- What stage directions do you need?

- How are you going to show the characters' personality and feelings through the dialogue?

Then write your playscript and perform it with your friends.

Using imagination or experience to write a poem

Think about one of the creatures in these pictures, or a
different one. Copy the chart into your book and write words
and phrases for each heading.

What it looks like	How it moves	What it sounds like	What it smells like	How it eats

2 How to write
a newspaper-style recount

1 Looking at the structure of newspaper-style recounts

1 You need **copymasters 6** and **7**.

Copymaster 6 shows a newspaper article which is all jumbled up! Cut up the sections and stick them on to **copymaster 7** in the right order.

2 This newspaper article is all jumbled up! Write down the letters of the sections in the right order.

Then write the correct heading next to each letter: **orientation**, **main body** or **reorientation**.

Racoon rescue

A new home... the new racoons Num Nigh, left, and Jumbo at Shepreth Wildlife Park

a The five-week-old animals were part of a large litter born in Scotland and had to be rescued after their owners were unable to look after the lot and needed to find new homes for some of them.

b Two baby racoons in need of a home have been given shelter at an animal sanctuary in Shepreth.

c The new arrivals will go into their own enclosure once they are ready to face the world in about eight weeks. Staff at the wildlife park will be happy to oblige visitors who ask to see them.

d Mr Willers said, "They have just started to toddle along as if they are drunk. They like climbing on to you with their long claws and like to be carried a lot."

e Jumbo and Num Nigh – meaning 'cute' and 'lovely' in the Thai language – arrived at Shepreth Wildlife Park just days ago. They were taken to the home of Terry Willers, one of the directors of the sanctuary, to be hand-reared.

3 Here is another jumbled news article. Again, write down the letters in the right order. Then write the correct heading next to each letter: **orientation**, **main body** or **reorientation**.

Born to be wild?

Keiko the too-tame killer whale in his new home

a

It is as hard for the keepers as it is for Keiko, and nothing is yet certain. But by summer, if all goes well, Keiko will be ready for his release into the open sea.

b

The problem turned out to be that Keiko was just too much of a pet! The world-famous mammal preferred to be hand-fed his favourite diet of herring, and couldn't work up the energy to chase wild salmon in the bay. His devoted keepers reported that Keiko was just like a child, and still much too tame. But all was not lost. To help prepare Keiko for a new life, new rules were set for his keepers. No eye contact, no more rubdowns or massages and no more dead fish!

c

Then, in the hope he would learn to adapt, he was given the freedom of an Icelandic bay surrounded by rugged mountains. In March this year, Keiko had his first go at swimming in the pure blue-green waters of the open sea. The gate to his floating pen was thrown open and he took a deep dive for the first time in more than 20 years.

d

First Keiko spent eight months in his own sea pen. His trainers said he was in great shape and his living space had grown from the size of one football pitch to that of twenty pitches. This was meant to help Keiko get used to the wild, but he stayed as tame as ever.

e

Last year Keiko the killer whale – the star of the 1993 film, *Free Willy* – was taken back to Iceland in a bid to give him his freedom after years spent in an aquarium.

1 Look at these photographs. What do you think each photo shows?

Make up a headline and a caption to go with each one. You can invent any extra details you like.

2 Read the texts below. They are all from the **orientation** part of a newspaper report.

Make up a headline for each one. If the article is serious, write a serious headline. If you think it is a 'human interest' story, try a more humorous or 'catchy' headline.

Hint!

To help with alliteration or rhyme in your headlines, use a thesaurus to explore the different words you could use.

a IN THE EARLY HOURS of yesterday morning, Tiddles, a pet tabby cat belonging to the Smith family, got stuck up a tall fir tree in the back garden of his south London home. He was rescued by a neighbour who used an extending ladder.

b Twenty firefighters and four fire engines attended a large fire at an Edinburgh hotel late last night. At about eleven o'clock at night, guests smelt smoke and raised the alarm, but it was too late. The kitchens were destroyed by a huge blaze. Nobody was hurt.

c Pupils in Year 4 at Sherwood Primary School in Nottingham met their Russian pen-pals this week. For more than two years, the children have been sending letters to pupils at a school near Moscow. A local charity paid for the class of twenty-five Russian boys and girls to come to England for a short holiday.

d A new teen-café opened in Cardiff city centre yesterday – and was an immediate hit! Gleaming with hi-tech chrome tables and painted in the latest fashion shades, *The Pop-Inn* aims to be a cool place for customers aged ten to eighteen to hang out in the evening and at the weekend.

3 Read these headlines. Which nursery rhyme or traditional tale do they come from?

1

Vicious knife-woman attacks three sightless mice

2

TWO BROTHERS MURDERED BY HUFFING PUFFER

3

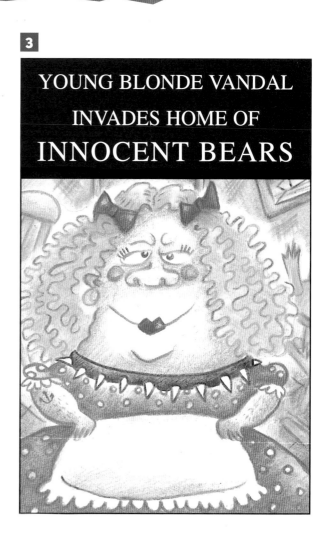

YOUNG BLONDE VANDAL INVADES HOME OF INNOCENT BEARS

4

WIDOW AND DOG IN STARVATION SCANDAL

Now write headlines of your own for these:

Humpty Dumpty

The Gingerbread Man

The Three Billy-Goats Gruff

Jack and Jill

Ding Dong Bell

1 Choose one of the photos that you wrote a headline and caption for (on page 20). Now write an orientation section to go with it. Make up the details of the story. Remember to include **who**, **what**, **where** and **when**.

2 Here are some headlines. Choose one 'serious' headline and one 'humorous' headline. Write an orientation section to go with each one. Remember to include **who**, **what**, **where** and **when**.

Humorous headlines

Escaped kangaroo gets hopping mad!

FIREWORK SHOW GOES OFF WITH A **BANG!**

Ghostly goings-on at Garrick Grange

Serious headlines

Scientist invents miracle drug

HEAVY RAIN CAUSES FLOODING

Escaped prisoner seen in Chester

Which headline was hardest to make up a story about? With your partner, discuss why it was difficult. Find out which one another group found the most difficult.

3 Now choose one of these 'catchy' headlines and do the same again. You will need to use your imagination to make up the story!

Friends forever

WHY ME?

WHO CARES?

HANDS UP!

Hello Kitty

LOOK WHO DROPPED IN!

_____
_____
_____
_____
_____
_____
_____
_____
_____
_____
_____
_____

Hint!

The **orientation** section of a newspaper article often tells us about **who**, **what**, **where** and **when**.

The **main body** of the article usually gives more information: it tells us about **why** and **how**.

1 Think of something that has happened at your school. Here are some examples:

- a concert;
- a visit from somebody special;
- a football match;
- a school trip;
- something funny or sad.

Copy this grid into your book. Leave plenty of space to write in.

Who?	What?	Where	When?	Why?	How?

Fill in the grid for your school event.

Your finished grid might look a bit like this:

Who?	What?	Where	When?	Why?	How?
Dave Winalot, the Arsenal striker – used to be a pupil at this school	Came to our school assembly	In the school hall	Three weeks ago	To present a cup to our school football team for winning the school league	He told us how important it is to practise every day

Writing a report

1 Read this report. In your book, write down a good title for it.

Then choose one of these headings for each section – **a**, **b**, **c** and **d**.

Headings Good food   Conclusion   Lovely lessons

There are only three headings, so you will need to make up a suitable heading for the other section.

Title _____

St Somebody's School is a junior school in a quiet part of Somewheretown. It is an excellent school with a lot of excellent qualities.

a _____

Teachers are friendly and kind. They keep the classrooms bright and warm. Lessons are very interesting. Every classroom has a computer for pupils to use when they need it. The reading corner is always full of new books.

b _____

The main playground is large and has two swings in it. Children are allowed to play football or netball at playtime and lunchtime. Bat and ball games can be played on the small yard. Pupils smile and laugh a lot.

c _____

School dinners are delicious. Children can choose what they want to eat. There is always fresh fruit on the tables. Children are shown how to choose and enjoy healthy meals. Dinner ladies never shout.

d _____

The school is a happy and safe place for children to spend their day. You can choose this school and be sure that your child will be well looked after and well taught.

Decide with a partner what the **purpose** of this report is. Who might read it?

2 Read these paragraphs which are all from reports.
For each paragraph, decide:

- What is the paragraph about?
- What kind of report is it from?
- What is the purpose of the report?
- Who might have written it?
- Who might read it?

1

Rede Hall is a working farm based on the agricultural life and practice of the 1940s and 1950s. It includes working Suffolk and Shire horses. Rare and minority breeds can also be seen. The use of farm implements, the growing of crops and the husbandry of livestock are all carried out in a traditional way.

3

Most sheepdogs have long, shaggy coats. Healthy animals of this breed are usually black and white, with thick, glossy fur. Their coat protects them against cold weather, so these dogs are usually able to live comfortably outdoors.

2

It is red and rather rusty, with a Manchester United Supporters' Club sticker on its saddle. It has a blue plastic saddle bag. When last seen, it was propped up against a fence outside the sweet shop.

4

In contrast, Dale's writing has very much improved and he has written some very imaginative poetry this term. He has also become much more interested in reading since he started reading our new 'Real Science' series. He still needs some encouragement in spelling, and must remember to check his work carefully.

Now write a short heading for each paragraph.

Writing clear and cohesive instructions

You need **copymaster 10**.

Choose one of the following to write instructions for. With a partner, discuss what the stages will be. Then plan your instructions using the copymaster.

How to play hopscotch
How to draw the hopscotch grid
How to play the game

How to send an email
How to switch on the computer and get into
  your mailbox
How to write and send a new message

**How to get a book from the school
  library**
How to go and choose the book
How to take the book out

**How to make a birthday card for
  a friend**
How to make the card
How to send it to your friend

What to do when you go swimming
How you get ready to swim
How you dive into the water safely

How to ride a horse
How to get onto the horse
How to make the horse trot

3 How to write

a poem about an imagined world

1 Poems with fantasy settings

1 Look at this picture. What can you see? With a partner, think of names for each thing.

Make up a name for this place and the people that live there. Write this in your book. Write about some other things you might find there.

2 Here are some more verses from 'The King of Quizzical Island'.

With a partner, decide which words and phrases tell us this is a fantasy setting.

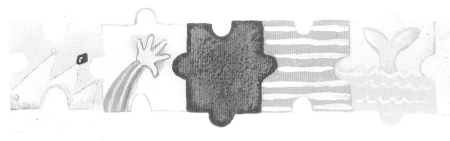

He sailed through waves as high as hills
For thirty days or more
Until at last, the ship was cast
On a higgledy-piggledy shore.

He found himself in a Jigsaw Land
Which lay there, all in pieces:
The blue bits might have been sea –
    or sky –
Or sheep, with ink-stained fleeces...

The green bits might have been grass –
    or leaves –
Or a snake, or a dragon's tail;
And the white bits might have been
    clouds – or snow –
Or the teeth of a smiling whale...

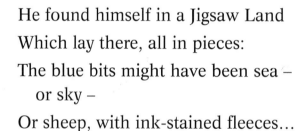

From 'The King of Quizzical Island' by Gordon Snell

In your book, describe some other things you might find in Jigsaw Land.

3 Read 'Dreams'. With a partner, decide which words and phrases tell us this is a fantasy setting.

Dreams

Beyond, beyond the mountain line,
The grey stone and the boulder,
Beyond the growth of dark green pine,
That crowns its western shoulder,
There lies that fairy land of mine,
Unseen of a beholder.

Its fruits are all like rubies rare,
Its streams are clear as glasses:
There golden castles hang in air,
And purple grapes in masses,
And noble knights and ladies fair
Come riding down the passes.

From 'Dreams' by Cecil Frances Alexander

In your book, describe some other things you might find in this fairy land.

1 Choose a word from this list to finish the simile. The first one has been done for you. Write them in your book.

fish   baby
wind   bird
feather   stone
snake   lion

1 swim like a ___fish___

2 cry like a _____

3 slither like a _____

4 float like a _____

5 sink like a _____

6 roar like a _____

7 fly like a _____

8 run like the _____

2 Finish these sentences with your partner. The first one has been done for you.

1 The monster was as tall as a house.

2 It was as strong _____

3 Its mouth was as wide _____

4 Its teeth were as sharp _____

5 Its arms were as long _____

Now draw a picture of this monster.

3 Finish these sentences by completing the similes. The first one has been done for you. Write them in your book.

1 The waves were as high as hills.

2 But the ship was as _____

3 The island was like _____

4 The forest was like _____

5 The castle was as _____

6 The towers were like _____

7 The guards looked as _____

8 They looked at me as if I was _____

9 I felt as _____

10 I ran like _____

Now tell the story to your partner.

1 Write a new chorus about the Jumblies. Copy this framework into your book and complete it.

> Far away, far away,
> Are the _____ where the Jumblies _____.
> Their _____ are _____, and their
> _____ are _____,
> And their favourite _____ is _____.

2 Here are some lines from another poem. They are in the wrong order. If you put them back in order, you will find they describe a fantasy setting.

The correct rhyme scheme should be:

red
red
blue
green
green
blue
pink
pink
blue

> Where the trees go Ping!
>
> All the mice go Clang!
>
> And the tea pots Jibber Jabber Joo.
>
> Where the cows go Bong!
>
> There's a Nong Nang Ning
>
> On the Ning Nang Nong
>
> And the monkeys all say Boo!
>
> And you just can't catch 'em when they do!
>
> On the Nong Ning Nang

Boo!

Write the poem in your book, in the correct order.

3 In your book, write two new choruses about the Jumblies. Use this framework or make up completely new choruses.

Remember to rhyme the first line with the third line, and the second line with the fourth line.

Far away, far away,
Are _____.
Their _____,
And _____.

Using expressive language

'Twas brillig, and the slithy toves
Did gyre and gimble in the wabe:
All mimsy were the borogoves,
And the mome raths outgrabe.

"Beware the Jabberwock, my son!
The jaws that bite, the claws that catch!
Beware the Jubjub bird, and shun
The frumious Bandersnatch!"

From 'Jabberwocky' by Lewis Carroll

1 Copy these verses into your book. Leave a gap between each line. Underline the nonsense words.

Replace the nonsense words with words from this list. Write them above the nonsense words.

slimy	silly	grumpy
revolting	talking–birds	monsters
snakes	pink pigs	dragon
slip and slide	whistled	scorpion
twilight	chilly	crazy
mud	crocodile	

2 Write these verses from 'Jabberwocky' in your book. Replace the nonsense words with real, expressive words.

3 Copy this table into your book. Describe an animal, a plant and a type of food in this world and in your imagined world.

Write some more if you have time.

	In this world	In my imagined world
Animal	e.g. Dogs are furry mammals with bushy tails and pointed snouts. They make very good pets.	e.g. Jabberwocks are scaly monsters with huge mouths and sharp claws. All the other creatures are afraid of them.
Plant		
Type of food		

Here is the complete 'Jabberwocky' poem. Plan the poem as a story in chapters. Use **copymaster 12**

Jabberwocky

'Twas brillig, and the slithy toves
Did gyre and gimble in the wabe:
All mimsy were the borogoves,
And the mome raths outgrabe.

"Beware the Jabberwock, my son!
The jaws that bite, the claws that catch!
Beware the Jubjub bird, and shun
The frumious Bandersnatch!"

He took his vorpal sword in hand:
Long time the manxome foe he sought –
So rested he by the Tumtum tree,
And stood awhile in thought.

And, as in uffish thought he stood,
The Jabberwock, with eyes of flame,
Came whiffling through the tulgey wood,
And burbled as it came!

One, two! One, two! And through and through
The vorpal blade went snicker-snack!
He left it dead, and with its head
He went galumphing back.

"And, hast thou slain the Jabberwock?
Come to my arms, my beamish boy!
Oh frabjous day! Callooh! Callay!"
He chortled in his joy.

'Twas brillig, and the slithy toves
Did gyre and gimble in the wabe;
All mimsy were the borogoves,
And the mome raths outgrabe.

By Lewis Carroll

Making notes

1 Help the King of Quizzical Island send some short messages home.

Write these sentences out as notes. The first one has been done for you.

1 I'm having an incredibly good time here in Vertical Land. It's really amazing – everything stands on its end! I don't know when we'll be coming home. I hope we can make it back for Christmas.

Having good time in Vertical Land. Everything on end. Don't know when coming home. Hope back for Christmas.

2 We have arrived at an island called Jigsaw Land. There are bits and pieces lying around all over the place. Please send me some really strong glue, so I can stick everything back together.

3 The seas are very rough at the moment. We've sailed through waves as high as hills! But we're finally on our way home. I've got lots and lots of presents for everyone.

2 Make notes from this letter. Draw a ship's logbook in your book to write the notes in.

Jigsaw Land

Monday, 10th March

Dearest Queen,

I have so much to tell you. Yesterday, my ship was cast on the higgledy-piggledy shore of the most incredible island. You wouldn't believe it! I later found out that the name of this place is Jigsaw Land. You see, everything on the island is in tiny little bits: the sky, the sea... even the grass!

My men and I have decided to put all the pieces back together. It'll probably take us ages and ages!

Must dash.

All my love,

King Quizzical II

Ship's logbook

Date: _____

_____

_____

_____

_____

4 How to write

an explanation of a process

① Looking at an explanation

Look at the labels on your explanation. They point out key features of explanations. Find more examples of each feature in the text.

1

present tense

Cleaning water

Water is essential for life. After it is used, however, water is often dirty and contaminated. For this reason, the process of cleaning water is very important.

sequence of steps

First of all, fresh water is pumped to a reservoir. Then it goes to a treatment works. It is held in tanks so that dirt sinks to the bottom. Next, the water is passed through filters that leave it completely clear. So that the water is also free of invisible bacteria, chemicals are added afterwards. Lastly, it is pumped to taps.

technical vocabulary

When it is flushed away, dirty water goes to a sewage works. Immediately, paper, plastic and other materials are sieved out. Then the sewage is held in settlement tanks so that solid matter settles as sludge, and can be taken out. The remaining liquid is passed through filters to remove pollution. Finally, the water is clean enough to release back into rivers and seas.

detailed information

The Earth cannot cope with the water pollution humans produce. Governments are introducing environmental protection laws, which demand efficient water-cleaning processes to protect the planet's water.

2

technical vocabulary

Recycling glass bottles

present tense

New glass bottles are made mainly of silica sand. The sand is melted in a furnace, at a very high temperature. Recycled glass bottles are made in a similar way, but cost less and use up fewer natural resources.

sequence of steps

The process begins when people take their used bottles and jars to a bottle bank. Next, the bottles and jars are taken by lorry to a recycling plant. At the plant, bottle tops and lids are removed. After that, the glass is crushed into small pieces.

detailed information

The crushed glass is then sent by lorry to a bottle factory. Here, it is mixed with a small amount of silica sand. It is then melted in a furnace, at a lower temperature than new glass. Finally, the hot liquid glass is drawn out of the furnace and fed into machinery that makes it into bottles.

Recycled glass is as pure and strong as new glass. Glass can be recycled many times without losing its quality.

3 Think of two differences between this explanation and a set of instructions. Write the differences in your book.

4

present tense

Making organic compost

To grow beautiful flowers or tasty vegetables, gardeners often put compost in their soil. Compost is produced by allowing vegetable matter to decompose naturally.

First the compost ingredients have to be collected. Any raw vegetable or plant material is suitable, including leaves, grass, vegetable peelings and fruit cores. To introduce helpful bacteria into the compost, some garden soil is also mixed in.

detailed information

Next, the compost mixture is put in a special composting bin, or piled up in a corner of the garden. The compost is then left alone for many months while nature does its work.

sequence of steps

Microbes, such as bacteria and fungi, soon begin to rot the vegetable material. As a side-effect, natural warmth is produced in the compost. This, in turn, helps to speed up the process. Eventually, natural decomposition transforms the waste vegetable material into soft brown compost.

technical vocabulary

Gardeners either dig the compost into the soil or spread it on the surface. Compost replaces nutrients in the soil, because it contains nitrogen and other important elements.

5 Think of two differences between this explanation and a set of instructions. Write the differences in your book.

Now think of two differences between the explanation and a non-chronological report. Write these in your book, too.

1 Use **copymaster 13**.

2 Look at **copymaster 13** again.

Match these sentences to the correct paragraph. Write each sentence in your book, followed by the number of the paragraph (1, 2, 3 or 4).

   a Bottle banks have different bins for clear, green and brown glass.

   b The crushed glass is then washed.

   c Bottles and jars are easy to collect and recycle.

   d Next, the glass is quickly cooled so that it stays clear.

   e On average, a quarter of glass bottles are recycled.

3 Use **copymaster 14**.

4 Look at **copymaster 14** again.

Match these sentences to the correct paragraph. Write each sentence in your book, followed by the number of the paragraph (1, 2, 3, 4 or 5).

   a It is important that the compost mixture has plenty of air in it.

   b The plants and vegetables in the compost contain lots of nutrients.

   c The microbes are then helped by insects and worms, which break down the vegetable material.

   d Gardeners like compost because it is a natural fertiliser.

   e When the process is finished, the compost smells like moist soil.

Here is a flow-chart to show the process of cleaning water.

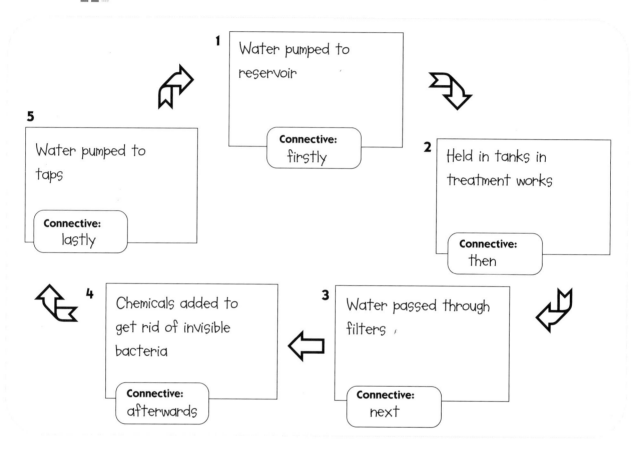

1 Here is the process of recycling glass bottles.

Write it as a flow-chart. Use **copymaster 15**.

People take their used bottles and jars to a bottle bank.

The glass is taken to a recycling plant.

The glass is crushed into small pieces

The crushed glass is sent to a bottle factory.

It is melted and made into bottles.

Choose chronological connectives from this list. Put them in the right boxes on **copymaster 15**.

finally   next   first of all   then   later

2 These pictures show the process of making chocolate. Use **copymaster 15**. Write out this process in the flow chart.

When you have finished, think of chronological connectives to put in the boxes on **copymaster 15**.

Cutting beans from a cocoa tree

Drying out the beans

Roasting the beans

Grinding the beans into cocoa butter

Cocoa butter is mixed with sugar and cream and made into bars of chocolate

3 Write a flow chart for another process (ask your teacher for ideas). Use a new copy of **copymaster 15**.

Think of different chronological connectives you can add. Use a thesaurus.

Hint!

Link an **action** to a **reason** with a **connective**.

| Action | | Connective | Reason |

The liquid is passed through filters in order to remove pollution.

You can change the order by putting the reason before the action. Put the connective at the beginning. Use a comma after the reason.

| Connective | Reason | | Action |

In order to remove pollution, the liquid is passed through filters.

1 Here are some sentences from an explanation about recycled paper.

Copy the chart into your book. Fill in the chart for each sentence. The first one has been done for you.

Action	Reason	Connective
Paper is recycled	it saves trees	because

1 Paper is recycled because it saves trees.

2 Old paper is soaked in water so that it becomes a soft pulp.

3 The pulp is put in a mixer to make it smoother.

4 The pulp is spread out on a frame so that there are no lumps.

5 The pulp is dried with a sponge because it is still very wet.

6 In order to keep it flat and smooth, the new paper is pressed under heavy weights.

2 Write some sentences of your own.
Think of an action, a reason and use connectives from your chart.

3 Write five sentences of your own.
Think of an action, a reason and use connectives from your chart. Write two with the reason *before* the action.

4 Here is an explanation about recycling paper.
Make the sentences longer by linking the actions to the reasons with connectives.
Write the new version in your book.

Recycling paper

Paper can be recycled. It saves trees and is good for the environment.

Old paper is shredded and soaked in water. It becomes a soft pulp. The pulp is drained and mixed in a blender. This makes it smoother. The pulp is spread out over a wooden frame. There should be no lumps. Then the pulp has to be blotted dry with a sponge. Any remaining moisture is absorbed. Heavy weights press the paper. It is kept flat and smooth.

5 Write five sentences of your own.
Think of an action, a reason and a connective for each one.
Write two with the reason *before* the action.

1 Copy this framework into your book. Use a whole page. Make notes for each section. Remember to complete the sub-headings and the title.

Title _____

Opening section (reason for the process)
Why _____ is important

Explanation of the process
What happens to the _____

First,

Then,

Next,

Afterwards,

Finally,

Closing section (additional information)
Extra information about _____

2 Copy this framework into your book. Use a whole page. Make notes for each section. Write the title and sub-headings in your book.

Title _____

Opening section (reason for the process)
Why _____ is important

Explanation of the process

Sub-heading _____

Sub-heading _____

Closing section (additional information)
Extra information about _____

ADDITIONAL SESSIONS

More about making notes

Hint!

Think about the **subject** and **purpose** of the text.

Think about the **key words**.

Decide which words are not essential.

1 Here are some sentences about wool-making. In your book, write them down as notes.

1 Most wool is made from short fibres that come from the fleece of a sheep.

2 Other animals also produce wool, such as goats and camels.

3 Nearly half of all the wool people use comes from Australia and New Zealand.

4 In spring, farmers shave off the sheep's fleece and then send it to woollen mills.

5 Wool is a very good material for clothes because it is strong and warm, and keeps its shape even when stretched.

2 With a partner, write three sentences about clothes. Now write them again as notes.

3   Here are two paragraphs about wool-making. In your book, write them out as notes.

At the mill, fibres from the fleece are separated into different lengths, then washed to remove grease and dirt. After washing, the fibres are straightened out. They are fed through a machine that combs them together into a soft, thin layer called a *web*. This process is known as *carding*.

Next, the web is split into thin strands. These are twisted together into long threads by spinning machines. The strands are spun several times, getting thinner and stronger each time.

4   With a partner, write five sentences about clothes. Now write them again as notes.

Writing up from notes

1 Swap with a partner the notes you made last time.
In your book, write these notes up as full sentences.

2 In your book, write these notes as full sentences.

> *Web split – thin strands. Twisted into long threads by spinning machine.*
> *Strands spun several times. Thinner + stronger each time.*
> *→ wool knitted into jumpers or woven into cloth.*
> *Wool – good for clothes. Strong, warm + keeps shape.*

3 Match these notes to the correct sentences.

Notes

1 When flushed, dirty water → sewage works
2 Environment protection laws – protect water
3 Used water dirty – cleaning important
4 Water from rivers + lakes → reservoir → treatment works
5 Water v. old – recycled natural processes.

a Water from rivers and lakes is first pumped to a reservoir, and then to a treatment works.

b Because used water is often dirty, the process of cleaning it is very important.

c When it is flushed away, dirty water is carried along a drainage system to a sewage works.

d The earth's water is very old and is constantly recycled by natural processes.

e Environment protection laws are passed to protect the planet's water.

Presenting information from different sources

 1 Use **copymaster 16**. Your teacher will tell you which material to research. Write your information like this:

Material	How it is recycled	Advantages of recycling	How to encourage recycling
Plastic bottles	1 Plastic bottles are taken to recycling centre. 2 Bottles made of different types of plastic are sorted into different piles. 3 . . .	Recycling plastic is much better for the environment than burying it.	Tell people why recycling plastic is important.

2 Think of a way to illustrate your information. Here are two examples:

a flow-chart

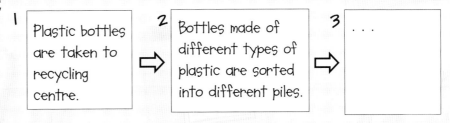

a labelled diagram

5 How to write
a story in chapters

1 Using chapters to organise longer stories

   1 Read this contents page. Talk about what you think happens in the story. Now use **copymaster 17**.

CONTENTS

When my big brother got the game I wanted
page 2

They wouldn't let me join in!
page 5

Just borrowing
page 7

Police!
page 10

Caught putting it back
page 13

The compromise
page 15

2 Read this contents page. Talk about what you think happens in the story. Now use **copymaster 17**.

1 Look at pictures 1, 2 and 4. Use **copymaster** 18.

Characters

Settings

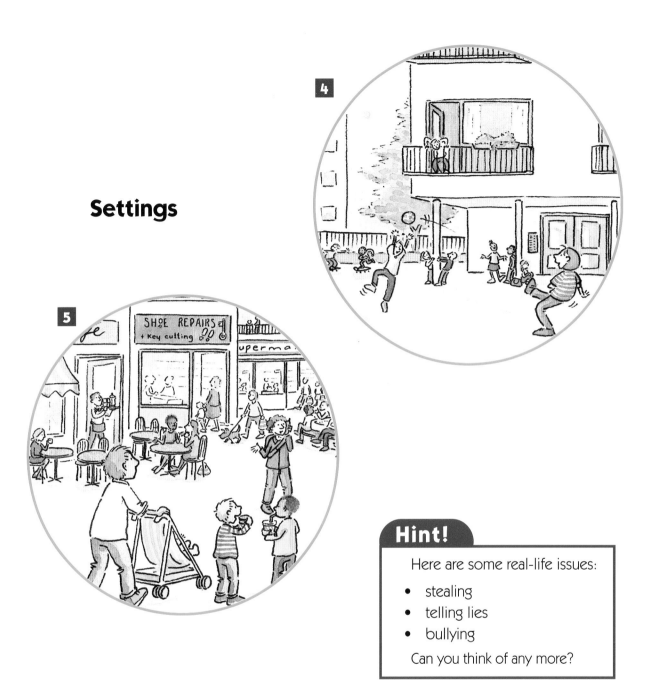

Hint!

Here are some real-life issues:

- stealing
- telling lies
- bullying

Can you think of any more?

2 Choose two characters and a setting from the pictures. Think of a real-life issue. (Use the Hint! if you want to.)

Now plan a story. Make notes about:

- the **problem**;
- the **events** in the story;
- the **resolution** of the problem.

1 Use **copymaster 19** to plan your story.

2 Copy this framework into your book. Use a whole page. Now plan your story. Add extra chapters if you want to. Do not write anything in the 'Link' box. (You will use it next time!)

Chapter 1	Characters: Setting: Problem: Issue:
	Link:
Chapter 2	Events:
	Link:
Chapter 3	Events:
	Link:
Chapter 4	Event: Climax:
	Link:
Chapter 5	Resolution:
	Link:

1   Work with a partner. Think of a TV series or a soap opera which you have seen recently. Think of examples of links from one episode to another. What makes the viewers want to watch the next episode?

2   Read this plan for part of a story called *Mystery in the Boat-house*. The author has planned some links between the chapters. Look at the example links that are given.

With a partner, find the links between chapter 3 and chapter 4 and write them down.

If you have time, make up what happens in chapter 5, and write some links between chapter 4 and chapter 5.

Mystery in the Boat-house

Chapter 1: The boat-house
Rob and Alex are staying by the sea with Grandad. Their family have come down to cheer Grandad up after his house was burgled. Rob (9) and Alex (8) are playing on the beach. Suddenly they hear a spooky whistling sound coming from an old boat-house. Nervously they open the door and tiptoe in.

Links between chapter 1 and chapter 2

Cliffhanger: What is the strange noise? Is it a ghost? No, it's a boy
              called Connor.
Characters: same, plus a new one
Setting: changes (beach → inside boat-house)

Chapter 2: Connor's den
Inside they find an older boy called Connor. He was making the whistling
sound as a joke. He has made a den upstairs in the boat-house, and the
boys spend a fun afternoon with him. He shows them some things he says
he has found on the beach. One of them is a strange old gold watch. Rob
has a feeling that he has seen it somewhere before.

Links between chapter 2 and chapter 3

Cliffhanger: Where has Rob seen the watch before? Grandad is wearing
              it in a photo.
Characters: same (but focus on Rob in chapter 3)
Setting: changes (boat-house → back at home)
Time: changes (daytime → night-time)

Chapter 3: The decision
That night Rob is lying in bed. Suddenly he remembers where he has
seen the watch. There is an old photo of Grandad downstairs and on his

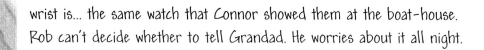

wrist is... the same watch that Connor showed them at the boat-house. Rob can't decide whether to tell Grandad. He worries about it all night.

Links between chapter 3 and chapter 4

Chapter 4: Moment of truth
Next morning at breakfast, Rob comes down to tell Grandad – but Grandad has gone fishing. Rob goes out, refusing to tell Alex where he is going. Alex is cross and secretly follows Rob. Rob goes to the boat-house and sneaks in. Nobody is about. He creeps upstairs to find the watch. Then he hears the door bang shut and Connor's voice shouting, "Hello?"

Links between chapter 4 and chapter 5

Chapter 5:

3   Look at your story plan from Session 3. Use the link boxes to plan links between your chapters.

ADDITIONAL SESSIONS

Writing an alternative ending

1 Copy this chart into your book. Fill it in with your ideas for a new ending to *Red Eyes at Night*.

When you have finished, write the last paragraph of your alternative ending.

My alternative ending	How this affects the way I see the characters and events

2 Copy this chart into your book. Fill it in with your ideas for two new endings to *Red Eyes at Night*.

Now choose one ending, and write the last paragraph for it.

Experimenting with poetry

1   Read these two limericks.

There was an Old Man with a beard,
Who said, "It is just as I feared! –
Two Owls and a Hen,
Four Larks and a Wren,
Have all built their nests in my beard!"

By Edward Lear

A woman while dining in Crewe,
Found a rather large mouse in her stew
Said the waiter, "Don't shout,
And wave it about,
Or the rest will be wanting one too!"

Anon

Copy the limericks into your book.

How many lines are there in each limerick?

Count how many beats there are in each line.

Underline the rhyming words in each limerick. What is the rhyme pattern?

2 Read 'From a Railway Carriage'.

Write down similarities and differences between this poem and 'Night Mail'.

Think about:

- what the poems are about;
- the rhyme patterns;
- the rhythm in the poems;
- the words the poets use to write about speed;
- how the poems make you feel.

FROM A RAILWAY CARRIAGE

Faster than fairies, faster than witches,
Bridges and houses, hedges and ditches,
And charging along like troops in a battle,
All through the meadows the horses and cattle:
All of the sights of the hill and the plain
Fly as thick as driving rain;
And ever again, in the wink of an eye,
Painted stations whistle by.

Here is a child who clambers and scrambles,
All by himself and gathering brambles;
Here is a tramp who stands and gazes;
And there is the green for stringing the daisies!
Here is a cart run away in the road,
Lumping along with man and load;
And here is a mill, and there is a river;
Each a glimpse and gone for ever!

By Robert Louis Stevenson

3 Read these **haiku**. Check the number of syllables in each one.

A series of haiku about the same subject is called a **renga**. Choose one of the haiku and write a second verse for it.

An Orca Whale Jumps

An Orca whale jumps
Sending a cry in the air,
Splashing water high.

By Rachel Kuhse
(Spring Green Elementary School, Wisconsin)

Falling Rain

Rain dripping down light
Twirling, whirling, coming fast.
Round and soft it comes.

By 'Jack' (2nd Grade, Minnesota)

Reflections on Pet Cats

Velvet and golden,
Softly purring predators
Only lend friendship.

Anon

Writing poetry

1 Copy this poem into your book. Complete the blanks with words from the list. Remember that the last word of each couplet should rhyme!

White Fields

In winter-time we go
Walking in the fields of _____;

Where there is no grass at all;
Where the top of every _____,

Every fence and every _____,
Is as white as white can be.

All across the fields there be
Prints in silver _____:

Pointing out the way we _____;
Every one of them the _____.

And our mothers always _____
By the footprints in the _____ ,

Where it is that children go.

By James Stephens

Word list
Snow
came
tree
know
filigree*
same
wall
Snow

* a fine thread

2 Here is a terrible limerick! Can you improve it?

Think about **rhymes**, **syllables** and **rhythm**. Look at the limericks on page 65 to help you.

Write the new version in your book.

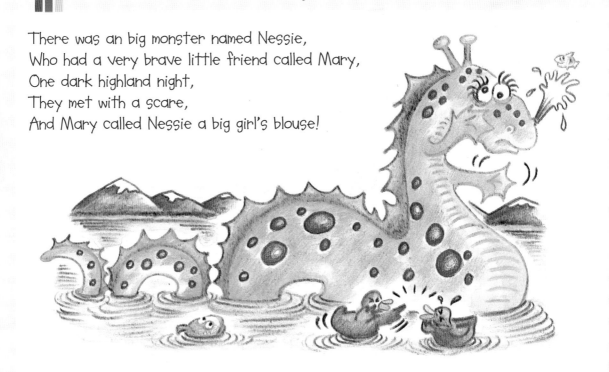

There was an big monster named Nessie,
Who had a very brave little friend called Mary,
One dark highland night,
They met with a scare,
And Mary called Nessie a big girl's blouse!

3 Read the haiku about cats on page 67. Think about an animal you know and write a list of words about it.

Copy this chart into your book. Put your words in the right columns. Use a thesaurus to find synonyms with different numbers of syllables.

Words with one syllable	Words with two syllables	Words with three syllables	Words with four syllables

Now use these words to write a haiku.

Remember to use five syllables in the first and third line, and seven syllables in the middle line.

6 How to write

a persuasive text

1 You need **copymaster 20** and four different coloured pens.

Use a different colour to mark each section:

> Introduction
> Argument
> Conclusion

Write the name of the section in the same colour.

Now look for **connecting words** (e.g. *because, so*) that are often used in this type of writing. Use a fourth colour to underline these.

What are the two **main points** of the argument? Write these in the boxes on the copymaster.

2 Here is a piece of persuasive writing. Read it carefully.

Decide which section is the **introduction**, the **argument** and the **conclusion**.

You should not eat too many sugary foods. Eating too much sugar is bad for your teeth and bad for your body.

Sugar is bad for your teeth because it causes tooth decay. Sugar on your teeth makes a sticky substance called plaque grow. This attacks your teeth and causes cavities. Therefore, eating too many sugary foods could lead to toothache, a trip to the dentist and even fillings! Your body does not need lots

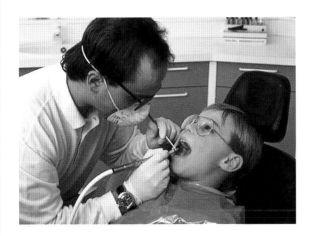

of sugar, so eating too much of it is bad for your health. If you eat sugary foods between meals then it can spoil your appetite for healthy food at mealtimes. It is important to try to eat lots of healthy foods instead that will give your body all the nutrients it needs.

As you have seen, too much sugar is bad for your health. So, try not to eat too many sugary foods!

In your book, write down the two main points of the argument. Write down the evidence that supports each point.

Write down any persuasive vocabulary in the text.

1 Here are six sentences to complete. Match the beginning and the ending and then link them together with the right connecting word. Write the complete sentences in your book.

Use these connecting words: 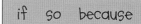 if so because

1	Your feet get wet	people need to rest.
2	It isn't safe to cross the road	they bark.
3	Dogs can't talk	it is frozen water.
4	Work is tiring	you jump in a puddle.
5	Snow is cold	they don't have wings.
6	Pigs can't fly	there is traffic coming.

2 With a partner, think of some reasons why it would be a good idea for children to have longer playtimes.

Write down the three best ideas that you think might convince your teacher!

Hint!

Remember to support your argument with **evidence** (reasons, facts and examples).

3 Read the following sentences. Put them in the right order so that the argument makes sense.

a That is why we should wear our own clothes to school.

b Children should be allowed to wear their own clothes to school.

c Our own clothes are more comfortable, so we feel happier wearing them.

d If we are more comfortable then we can concentrate better.

4 Persuade your teacher that you should be allowed to eat sweets in class. Try to think of some reasons why this would be a good idea.

Write the three best reasons out as sentences.

> ### Hint!
>
> - Plan a list of ideas and evidence to support your argument.
> - Start with the most important point.
> - Use connecting words (e.g. *so, because, if, however, therefore*).

5 Read the writing below. It is an argument in favour of selling ice-cream at school, but the sentences are in the wrong order.

Put the sentences in the right order so that the argument makes sense. Add connecting words to link the points of the argument.

> It would be good for us as well as delicious. Children would bring more money from home to buy them and we could raise money for the school. We should sell ice-creams at lunchtime in the summer. On hot days, the ice-cream would help to keep us cool.

6 With a partner, prepare and write an argument.

Here are some ideas for your writing:

> Children should be given more pocket money.
> There should be more school holidays.
> Walking or cycling to school is better than coming by car.

1 Read these two pieces of persuasive writing (there is another one on page 75).

> We need more computers at school. Children should work on the computer every day. In our class, there is only one computer, so everyone has to wait for a turn to use it. If we had more computers then we would not have to wait so long for a turn.

Which of these sentences would make the best opening statement?

   a Computers are fun to work on.

   b All children should have a computer of their own at school.

   c We need more computers at school.

   d Children should work on the computer every day.

If children could choose their own bedtimes then they would stay up too late. This would make them tired the next day so they would not concentrate at school. Children would like to stay up later because they would like to watch more TV. However, if they chose their own bedtimes they would watch so much TV that they would not be able to get up on time the next morning.

Which of these sentences would make the best opening statement?

a Children should choose their own bedtimes.

b Children like watching TV.

c Children do not like getting up in the morning.

d Children should not choose their own bedtimes.

Now think of some points to add to the arguments – or to argue the **opposite** point of view!

2 Read this piece of persuasive writing. What do you think is its main purpose? Write an opening statement.

If our school had a swimming pool then we would all learn to swim more quickly because we could have swimming lessons at school whenever we wanted to. We would save time because we would not have to travel to the pool in town, so we would have more time for work. We would also be able to have swimming lessons in the summer instead of having P.E. outside and then we would feel much cooler on hot days.

Can you think of any other points that the writer could have made? Write down any that you can think of.

Hint!

Remember that you need to grab your reader's attention so keep the introduction **brief** and think of a **dramatic** opening sentence.

3 Read this piece of persuasive writing. Then write an introduction and a conclusion for it.

Hint!

End your conclusion with something **memorable**!

There are many things that children could be doing after school that are even more valuable than homework. Children are tired after school because they have been working all day. It is important for children to rest after school and to have time to play and to meet up with friends. However, if they have lots of homework to do then there is no time to rest or play. This means that children are often tired at school the next day. To keep fit and healthy, people have to be active and take exercise. This is another reason why children should not be indoors all the time doing homework but should have time to play in the fresh air.

Do you agree with the writer? Can you think of some points to add to the argument – or to argue the **opposite** point of view?

Writing an advert

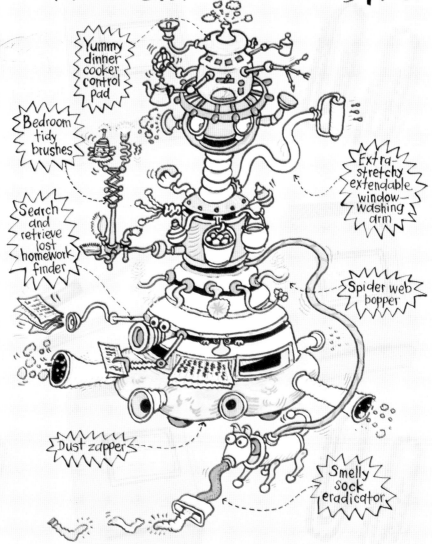

Invent your own fantasy machine. It could be for doing homework, making ice-cream, printing money or whatever you like.

Draw your machine and label its different parts.

Write an advert to persuade someone to buy it.

Writing advertising slogans and jingles

Here is Willy Wonka talking about his amazing new chewing gum.

"My dear sir!" cried Mr Wonka, "when I start selling this gum in the shops it will change *everything*! It will be the end of all kitchens and cooking! There will be no more shopping to do! No more buying of meat and groceries! There'll be no knives and forks at mealtimes!

No plates! No washing up! No rubbish! No mess! Just a little strip of Wonka's magic chewing gum – and that's all you'll ever need at breakfast, lunch and supper! This piece of gum I've just made happens to be tomato soup, roast beef, and blueberry pie, but you can have almost anything you want!"

You are going to invent adverts for some of Willy Wonka's new sweets. Read the description of the sweet first. Here is one of them:

INVISIBLE CHOCOLATE BARS FOR EATING IN CLASS

Imagine you are advertising the sweet on the radio. What could you say about it? What would make children buy it?

A good way to start is by thinking about why **you** would want to buy the sweet.

Here are some ideas for a slogan or jingle:

Chomp your choc in secret!

Don't break the rule, be cool at school with Wonka's invisible chocolate!

Remember that **rhymes** and **alliteration** help to make slogans catchy and interesting.

When you have written your slogan or jingle, illustrate it with a picture of the sweet. Choose from the list below.

If you have an idea for a sweet of your own, write an advert for that too.

LICKABLE WALLPAPER FOR NURSERIES

HOT ICE CREAMS FOR COLD DAYS

FIZZY LIFTING DRINKS

EXPLODING SWEETS FOR YOUR ENEMIES

LUMINOUS LOLLIES FOR EATING IN BED AT NIGHT

CAVITY-FILLING CARAMELS – NO MORE DENTISTS!

From *Charlie and the Chocolate Factory* and *Charlie and the Great Glass Elevator* by Roald Dahl

PUBLISHED BY THE PRESS SYNDICATE OF THE UNIVERSITY OF CAMBRIDGE
The Pitt Building, Trumpington Street, Cambridge, United Kingdom

CAMBRIDGE UNIVERSITY PRESS
The Edinburgh Building, Cambridge CB2 2RU, UK
40 West 20th Street, New York, NY 10011-4211, USA
10 Stamford Road, Oakleigh, VIC 3166, Australia
Ruiz de Alarcón 13, 28014 Madrid, Spain
Dock House, The Waterfront, Cape Town 8001, South Africa

http://www.cambridge.org

© Cambridge University Press 2001

First published 2001
Reprinted 2001

Printed in the United Kingdom at the University Press, Cambridge

Typefaces Concorde, Frutiger, ITC Kabel   *System* QuarkXPress®

A catalogue record for this book is available from the British Library

ISBN 0 521 80545 7

Cover design by Traffika Publishing Ltd
Design by Angela Ashton
Picture research by Callie Kendall
Artwork chosen by Heather Richards
Illustrations by Barry Ablett, Peter Bailey, Beccy Blake, Eikon, Louise Alexandra Ellis, Amanda Hall, Cecilia Johansson, Sally Kindberg, Stephen Lambert, Sami Sweeten, Thomas Taylor and Caroline Williams

We are grateful to the following for permission to reproduce text extracts:
A Camp to Hide King Alfred © Roy Apps, 1997, reproduced by permission of Hodder and Stoughton Limited; *The Saga of Leif Erikson* © Roy Apps, 1998, reproduced by permission of Hodder and Stoughton Limited; 'Racoon Rescue', reproduced by kind permission of the Cambridge Evening News; 'Born to be wild?', reproduced by kind permission of thenewspaper.org; 'The King of Quizzical Island' © Gordon Snell, reproduced by permission of John Johnson Limited, on behalf of Gordon Snell; 'On the Ning Nang Nong' © Spike Milligan, reproduced by permission of Spike Milligan Productions Ltd; *Charlie and the Chocolate Factory* © Roald Dahl, published by Penguin Books Ltd, reproduced by permission of David Higham Associates.

We are grateful to the following for permission to reproduce photographs and illustrations:
9, © Martyn F. Chillmaid/Robert Harding Picture Library; 17 top, © Scott Cazamine/www.osf.uk.com; 17 bottom, © R. Austing/FLPA; 18, reproduced by kind permission of the Cambridge Evening News; 19, © C. Carvalho/FLPA; 20 top, © T. Waltham/Robert Harding Picture Library; 20 bottom, 24, 25, 26, 28 (middle and bottom), 74, © www.johnwalmsleyphotos.co.uk; 23, © PA Photos; 27 (both), © G. T. Andrewartha/FLPA; 28 top © David Lomax/Robert Harding Picture Library 43, © Tick Ahearn; 44, © Mike J. Thomas/FLPA; 47 © Cadbury Limited; 49 left, © Robert Harding Picture Library; 49 right, © Sally Morgan/Ecoscene; 52 © Ken Day/FLPA; 53, © Corbis Images; 66, © Milepost 92$\frac{1}{2}$; 67, © Gerard Lacz/FLPA; 68, © David Hosking/FLPA; 71, © Robert Harding Picture Library; 78, © Quentin Blake, 1995, from *Charlie and the Chocolate Factory*, by Roald Dahl (Puffin 1995), reproduced by permission of Penguin Books Ltd.

Every effort has been made to trace all copyright holders. If there are any outstanding copyright issues of which we are unaware, please contact Cambridge University Press.